Some of the mat
used in the expe
described in this

SCIENCE
EXPERIMENTS

IRON FILINGS

Through simple and safe experiments children can learn about the principles of magnetism and electricity. This book also gives some of the historical background to this science and a description of modern day applications.

Acknowledgments

The authors and publisher would like to thank the following for extra photographs used in this book; page 20 Squadron Leader B E Russell and The National Meteorological Library; page 41 Popperfoto.

First Edition

© LADYBIRD BOOKS LTD MCMLXXXII

Magnets and Electricity

by JOHN and DOROTHY PAULL

illustrated by PETER ROBINSON

photographs by TIM CLARK

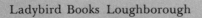

Ladybird Books Loughborough

Magnets

Magnets are curious things. They possess a power which draws some kinds of metals towards them. This strange power is important to our everyday lives. There are different shaped magnets in toys and games, and as well as having a novelty and fun value, the power of magnets is vital to electrical gadgets like refrigerators, televisions and telephones.

Not all magnets are man-made. Magnetic rocks occur naturally in many parts of the world. There is a legend about the first discovery of magnetic rocks. Many centuries ago in Crete, an old shepherd named Magnus was up in the hills tending his sheep. Magnus had an old willow staff, tipped with iron. As his sheep nibbled the grass he passed the time by prodding and pushing his staff through a heap of stones at the bottom of a shallow pool. Suddenly he felt his staff pull as if it was caught by something heavy. The old shepherd pulled out the staff and a rock was sticking to the iron tip. Magnus had discovered *lodestone* (also called *magnetite*), a rock containing magnetic iron.

Magnus discovers lodestone

4

In the 12th century, the Chinese discovered that lodestone could help guide sailors back to land if boats were caught in thick, swirling fog. Chinese sailors hung lodestone on lengths of cord on the ships' bows. When the lodestone came to rest, the mysterious stone always pointed North and South.

Lodestone was used as a simple compass

During the reign of Elizabeth I, Sir William Gilbert (1544-1603) studied magnetism and helped others to understand the strange qualities of lodestone. His studies became famous and he is now known as the 'Father of Magnetic Science'.

Finding out about magnetic power

You can experiment with magnets like a scientist. When you experiment, always take your time and work carefully. Sometimes things will not work out as you expect. Check what you have done. Remember, in science there is always a reason when your results are not what you expected.

Sir William Gilbert, like all scientists, wrote notes and drew diagrams about his experiments. You should also keep a notebook of your scientific investigations.

Let's find out which substances
a magnet will pick up

This experiment helps to sort out which materials are attracted by magnetic forces.

Things you need

a small magnet

an old shoe or shirt box

a pencil and notebook

a collection of different small items, including coins, screws, nails, plastic buttons, sand, a small piece of wood, a knife and a fork.

What you do

(1) Put all your objects in the box.

(2) Take two pages in your notebook and write on one, *ATTRACTED TO MAGNET*, and on the other, *NOT ATTRACTED TO MAGNET*. This is your checking system.

(3) Bring your magnet close to each object in the box. If any article is attracted to the magnet, write its name or description under that heading. If something in the tray does not stick to the magnet, then write it on the other page.

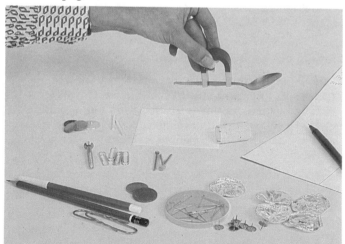

When you have tested everything, look at the two lists. You will notice that magnets strongly attract things made of iron and steel. Nickel and cobalt are other metals which are attracted to magnets.

What happened when you put the magnet in the sand? Did you pick up anything? Sometimes there are particles of magnetite in sand. Can the magnet attract a paper clip, a ball bearing, a coin, a milk bottle top, a hair grip? Test as many things as you can.

WARNING: Be careful *not* to take your magnet near to clocks or watches.

Let's find out what happens when two magnets are brought together

What you do

(1) Hold a bar magnet in each hand and slowly bring them together. What happens? Do they push each other away? Do they pull towards each other?

(2) When you have done this a few times, put the two magnets on a table and gently push them towards each other. What happens? Do they twist and turn and attract each other?

You will notice that magnets are strongest at each end, and these areas are called the *poles*. Some magnets have the poles painted a different colour from the rest of the magnet.

Did you notice how the magnets sometimes pushed each other away, and sometimes they pulled together? Each magnet has a *South pole* and a *North pole*. When magnets are brought together, the same kinds of poles push the magnets apart, and opposite poles pull them together.

Let's find out about magnetic fields

Magnets, through their poles, exert strong invisible forces. Scientists call this power the *Magnetic Field*. We can prove that Magnetic Fields exist.

Things you need

a yogurt container
3 bar magnets
pin
4 empty matchboxes

iron filings
(enough to quarter fill the container)
sheets of white paper
elastic band

What you do

(1) Make a lid for the yogurt container out of paper and fix it to the pot with an elastic band. Prick a number of small holes in the paper cover with the pin so that the filings drop through when you shake the container, rather like a pepper pot.

(2) Rest each corner of a sheet of white paper on four matchboxes and put one magnet underneath the centre.

(3) Sprinkle on the iron filings. Tap the paper gently and see how the filings form patterns round the magnet shape.

8

Lines of Force from three bar magnets

The lines in the pattern are called *Lines of Force*. Can you see where Lines of Force begin and end? Notice how they come from the poles. What happens when you put two magnets underneath the paper and sprinkle iron filings on top? Now try with three magnets (see above).

Let's find out through which different materials magnets will work

Things you need

wooden coffee table	paper clips
plastic tray	4 empty matchboxes
biscuit tin lid	bar magnet
jam jar	horseshoe magnet

What you do

(1) Hold one of the magnets underneath the table and put some paper clips on the topside of the table. Move the magnet about. Can you make the paper clips move? Try this with the other magnet.

9

(2) Rest the tray on the four matchboxes with the magnet underneath. Put paper clips on the tray and repeat the experiment.

(3) Try the same thing with the tin lid. What happens?

(4) Now put some paper clips in a jam jar and see if you can make them move using a magnet on the outside of the jar.

(5) Half fill the jar with water and try the experiment again. Does magnetism pass through glass and water?

Make a list in your notebook of materials through which magnetic forces pass. You could make a football game or farmyard game. Draw and colour in small players or animals (about 4 or 5 cm high) on thin card. Cut them out and stick them onto pieces of cork about 2 cm thick. On the underside of each cork base push in a drawing pin.

Now prepare a large piece of thick cardboard and paint it. This will be your football field or farmyard. Stick 2 or 3 empty matchboxes down each underneath side of your cardboard, to raise it from the floor or tabletop. Tie a small magnet to a length of stick and you are now ready to play your game. The magnet will move the players or animals because the magnetism will pass through the cardboard and the drawing pins will be attracted by the magnet.

It is easy to compare the strengths of magnetic fields of different magnets.

Let's find out which is the strongest magnet in your collection

Things you need
a selection of different sized and shaped magnets
a sheet of cm squared paper
paper clips

What you do
(1) Spread out a box of paper clips on a table top. Count how many clips each magnet will pick up before the clips start dropping off. Do it so that the clips attach to each other like a chain. You will find that the strongest magnet will pick up the most paper clips.

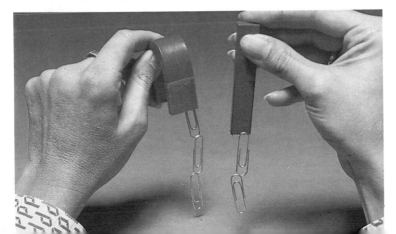

(2) Check your results another way. Lay a sheet of cm squared paper on a table and put a magnet at the bottom and a paper clip at the top of the sheet. Bring the first magnet slowly towards the clip until it moves towards the magnet. If the space between the magnet and paper clip was 3 cm before the magnet attracted the clip, then that distance can be compared with the other magnets. Again, the strongest magnet will attract a paper clip from the greatest distance.

(3) Make a chart in your notebook showing how each different magnet attracted paper clips from different distances. This chart will show you which is your strongest magnet. Is it your biggest magnet?

Can you make a chain of clips with your strongest magnet? Is it possible to make a bridge of paper clips between the poles of two magnets? What is the biggest bridge you can make? Can two magnets put together lift twice as many paper clips as one magnet? (Be careful — don't drop your magnet!)

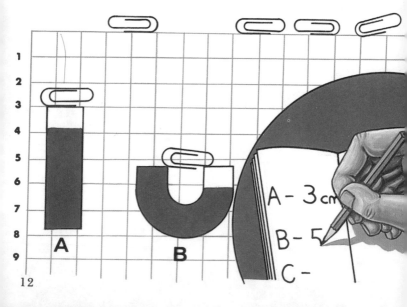

You can make other magnets from one strong magnet.

Let's find out how to make a magnet

Things you will need

1 bar magnet
paper clips
1 steel nail or long steel needle
iron nail

What you do

Use something made from steel in this experiment because iron will not stay magnetised but steel will remain magnetically charged for a long time. Take a steel nail or needle and carefully stroke it with one pole of your magnet, always moving it in the same direction and making sure to lift the magnet well clear of the nail at the end of each stroke. After about 5 minutes of stroking, test the nail with some paper clips. You have made a brand new magnet. You can make a selection of magnets of all shapes and sizes.

Has your magnet weakened? After you have made a few magnets, check your old one's strength by picking up some paper clips.

You can make hundreds of new magnets from your old one and it will not affect its strength at all. Magnets do lose their power to attract steel and iron, though, if dropped onto a hard floor or if hit hard with a hammer. Look after all your magnets by putting iron nails across the poles when you are not using them. The nails keep the magnets strong and are called *keepers*.

Scientists tell us that a magnet is made of millions and millions of microscopic magnets. You can cut a magnet and make two or more from it. The more you cut a magnetised rod, the more magnets you make.

You can use a magnetised needle to make a simple compass similar to those used centuries ago by Chinese sailors.

Let's find out how to make a compass

Things you will need

a large storage jar

a sheet of thin card

a saucer of water

10 cm of cotton

a flat piece of cork

a magnetised needle

What you do

(1) Cut out a 6 cm square of paper card and push a magnetised needle through it (see diagram). Mind your fingers as you push the needle!

(2) Make a small hole in the top of the card and tie the length of cotton to it.

(3) Tie the card and needle to a pencil and rest it across the top of a large storage jar. The storage jar will prevent wind or air affecting the movement of the needle.

Why does a compass point north? Early sailors used the lodestone as a guide at sea but did not really understand what made the magnetic stone point north. Sir William Gilbert said the earth itself was a giant magnet. He made a huge model of the earth and showed that magnets always point north, no matter where they are placed on the earth's surface. Scientists now have worked out that compasses point to a place called Baffin Island, in the northern hemisphere, and to the Antarctic, in the southern hemisphere. These are the *Magnetic North* and the *Magnetic South*.

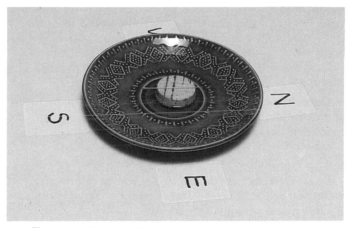

The magnetised needle turns the cork to a north/south position

Mark a large sheet of paper in felt pen with the points of the compass (N/S/E/W). Gently lift the jar and rest it on the middle of the compass drawing. Turn the paper until the north mark lies in the same direction as the pointed end of the magnetised needle. You now have a compass.

Another way is to rest a magnetised needle on a small piece of floating cork in a saucer of water. The magnet will turn the cork in a north/south position.

Static electricity

Sometimes, at night time, especially during autumn when the weather is cold and dry, your hair crackles when you pull your jumper over your head. Have you seen sparks fly when you take off a nylon shirt or blouse in a darkened bedroom? Or felt a tingle up your spine when you slide across a plastic covered car seat? Strange and curious happenings like these are not unusual. They are caused by *static electricity*; a charge produced by rubbing two different materials against each other.

Early man must have wondered about odd and weird happenings in nature caused by static electricity. Thales (640-546 BC), a Greek philosopher, discovered that when he rubbed amber (fossilised tree resin) with his clothes, it attracted small pieces of wood, the way lodestone attracts iron. The word *electricity* comes from the Greek word *elektron* which means amber.

Over the next 2000 years little progress was made in the study of static electricity. Sir William Gilbert, who was renowned for his work with magnets, also investigated static electricity, and noticed that other materials attracted certain objects when rubbed with a dry cloth.

Static electricity is fascinating. It is easy to investigate at home because it is safe and you do not need any special equipment. A plastic comb will do.

Sir William Gilbert explains his work to Queen Elizabeth I

Let's find out:
Experiments with Static Electricity

Sticking a newspaper to a wall

Things you will need
a large sheet of newspaper
a flat dry wall
a ruler

What you do

Rest the sheet of newspaper on a wall and rub it hard with a ruler. What happens when you take your hands away? Does the newspaper fall to the floor? If the conditions are right, the paper will stick to the wall on its own.

Fun with wool

Things you will need
a balloon
2 lengths of wool yarn

What you do

Lay two long pieces of wool yarn on a table and rub them lengthways with an inflated balloon. Then hold up both pieces of wool at one end and keep them about 6 cm apart. What happens? Can you get the same result with string?

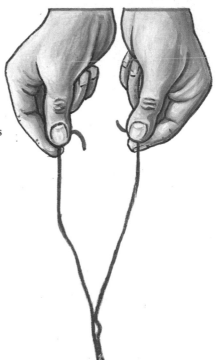

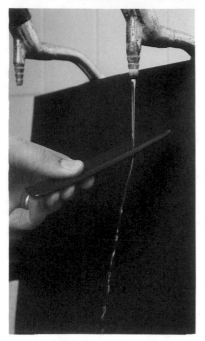

Bending water

Things you will need
a cold water tap
a plastic comb

What you do

Turn on a cold water tap in the kitchen until you get a fine, thin stream of water. Comb your hair and bring the plastic comb close to the tap water. What happens? Can you see the water 'bend'? Try rubbing some other objects. Do they make the water 'bend'?

The water bends towards anything that is charged with static electricity, but remember, a cold, *dry* day produces the best results.

Attracting paper with a comb

Things you will need
a plastic comb
some tiny pieces of paper

What you do

Cut several tiny pieces of paper and lay them on a table. Comb your hair a few times and bring the comb close to the paper. What happens? Is the paper attracted to the comb? Can you pick up some of the paper with the comb?

Try the experiment again with some small pieces of cork. How many pieces of cork can you pick up with the comb? Try a few other materials.

Moving a table tennis ball

Things you will need
a plastic comb
some woollen material
a table tennis ball

What you do

Charge a plastic comb by rubbing it hard with the woollen cloth and bring it close to a table tennis ball resting on a table. What happens?

The coin in the jar trick

Things you will need
a coin
a jam jar
a matchstick
a comb

What you do

This is a fun experiment and will amaze your friends. Stand a coin on its edge and rest a matchstick across the top of it.

Then carefully put a jam jar over the coin. Charge the comb as before and bring it close to the glass. The matchstick will be attracted to the comb and fall off.

Remember, all these experiments work best in cold dry conditions.

Lightning at Bassingbourn in Cambridgeshire

Thunder and lightning

Static electricity can cause problems. When the sky goes black, and fork lightning flashes and cracks above our heads, we feel the effects of static electricity on a massive and frightening scale. Some houses are protected from bolts of lightning by *lightning conductors* attached to their roofs. The metal strips attract the lightning and channel it safely into the ground.

Early man probably thought that the sky flashes were the anger of the sky spirits. Much later, man believed that thunder was caused by huge violent explosions of different gases behind the clouds.

Benjamin Franklin (1706-1790) was an American scientist who was intrigued and fascinated by lightning. One day, in 1752, he made a big kite and tied a piece of silk to the kite's string. He tied a big iron key to the silk. When the storm clouds gathered, he flew his kite. The lightning struck the metal key and big sparks of electricity flew off it. This way of proving that lightning is electrical energy was so dangerous that the experiment has never been repeated. Sometimes, sadly, you read in the newspapers of people and animals being struck dead by lightning bolts.

A cumulo-nimbus thundercloud, with its typical anvil-shaped top, may tower to over 30 thousand feet (2730 m)

The high speed movement of water droplets inside thunderclouds produces electricity. The difference in voltage between the top and bottom can reach 100 million volts. At this point there is a discharge which results in the flash we know as lightning. The heat produced expands the air and the sound of thunder is heard.

Electricity

Imagine a world suddenly without electricity. Nearly all machines would stop and cities and towns would be plunged into darkness and panic. It would be disastrous.

Electrical power is a marvel of the twentieth century and a tribute to many great thinkers and experimenters throughout history who were fascinated by this amazing source of power.

Electricity is a type of energy. When this special energy is at rest and not moving, scientists call it *static electricity*. If the energy moves quickly through something, it is called *current electricity*.

Electric currents cannot start on their own. To make something work by electricity there must be a source of power, such as a power station or battery, wires down which the current flows, and an appliance, like a bulb. This arrangement is called a *circuit*.

In the next few pages there are some experiments you can do at home and a list of items you can collect or buy.

When you experiment with electricity you can safely use torch or radio batteries up to 12 volts in power (batteries are measured in volts and this information is written on the side of all batteries).

For our experiments, batteries of no more than 4½ volts are strong enough to do all we need. The mains supply at home is at 240 volts and is *very* dangerous.

Never play with power points.

Do not use power points for experiments.

Do not use car batteries. They contain acid and are *dangerous*.

Let's look at the equipment you need to gather together for the investigations into electricity.

Wire
Electrical wire is easy to get hold of in quite large quantities. Collect a variety of metal wires. For most of the experiments use thin wire covered with cotton, silk, wire that is enamelled or covered with plastic. Size 28 standard wire gauge is the best for our purposes.

Wire Cutters
Ordinary pliers are fine, though wire cutters will make baring the wire ends easier.

Batteries
The battery is the source of electrical power. The ones that we will use produce small amounts of electricity big enough to light small bulbs but not enough to hurt us. You will not get an electric shock doing our experiments. Buy single cell and double cell batteries of strength 1½v, 3v and 4½v. Get as many as you can. Store them in a kitchen refrigerator when you are not using them. This helps to preserve their life.

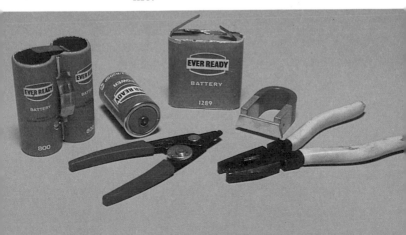

Bulbs	Electric current is measured in amperes (amps). The size of the current recommended to pass through a bulb is written on it. So you should buy torch bulbs with 2.5v, 0.5 amps marked on them. This means that a voltage of 2.5v will make a current of 0.5 amps pass through the bulb and light it. Anything stronger could burn the bulb out very quickly.
Bulb Holders	These plastic screw bases for the torch bulbs are on sale in electrical shops.
Switches	Small switches are available from your local radio spares shop.
Magnets	Bar magnets and a large horseshoe magnet.
'Odds and ends'	Large cork, drawing pins, needles, pins, torch, tin tacks, jam jar, pieces of wood, nails, darning needles.
Electrician's screwdriver	Small and narrow screwdrivers are ideal for our work with batteries and bulbs. You can buy them from any hardware or DIY shop.

Once you have gathered all these things, put them into a cardboard box. You used a notebook to keep records of your experiments with magnets and static electricity, so carry on in the same book with your electricity investigations. Later, a special shorthand will be explained and this will help you to keep notes more easily.

Let's find out how to light a small torch bulb

Things you will need
3v and 1½v batteries
some strands of thin wire cut into 10 cm lengths
a small torch bulb
a screw bulb holder
a pair of wire strippers
an electrician's screwdriver
(some Sellotape may be useful to hold connections)

What you do
(1) Take two pieces of electrician's wire and bare the ends with the strippers.

(2) Screw each wire to the bulb holder.

(3) Screw in the small bulb and fix the wires to the metal terminals of the 3v battery. Make sure that one wire goes to one terminal, and the other wire to the second battery terminal (see diagram).

(4) When all connections are complete the bulb will light up brightly.

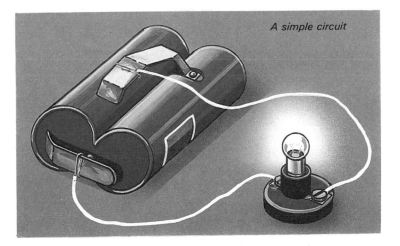

A simple circuit

You have now made a simple circuit, which means that the electricity is flowing from the battery, through the wire and into the bulb, then back through the other wire to the battery. If this circuit is broken somewhere, for example, if a wire is loose, then the bulb will not light. Always check the connections first if the bulb does not shine.

(5) When you have done this, take the bulb out of the holder. Using the two-celled 3v battery, one 10cm strand of wire and the bulb, can you now make a circuit and light the bulb?

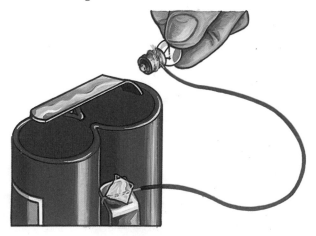

You will miss having a bulb holder and you may find it easier if you stick one end of the wire to the battery terminal with a small piece of Sellotape. Wrap the other end of the wire round the screwlike base of the torch bulb so that it grips the bulb tightly. There is a blob of solder on the bottom of the bulb. Sit this on the battery terminal and the bulb should light if the connections are right.

Can you repeat this experiment with a single-cell 1½v barrel battery? Does the length of wire in the circuit affect the brightness of the bulb? Is the bulb brighter with short strands of wire? Is the bulb dull if you use thick wire in the circuit? Can you make the bulb light using ONLY a pair of scissors, a bulb and either of the batteries?

A *switch* stops or allows electricity to flow into appliances like our bulb. You can buy small switches from a shop but it's fun to make your own switch.

Let's find out how to make a switch

Things you will need

electrical wire   paper clips
bulb   3v battery
bulb holder   drawing pins
a piece of wood about the size
  of a matchbox

What you do

(1) Connect two wires to the terminals of a battery then connect one of these wires to the bulb.

(2) Bare the end of the other piece of wire and wind it round a drawing pin.

(3) Hook the end of an opened out paper clip round another drawing pin and attach a third piece of wire between this and the remaining bulb connection. Press the pin into the block of soft wood.

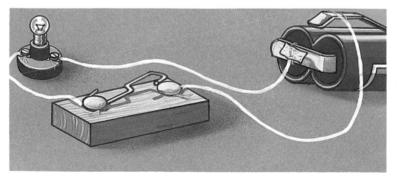

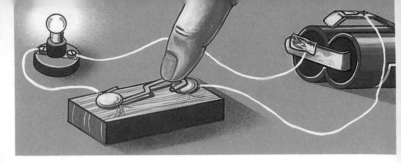

(4) Move the paper clip so that it touches the other drawing pin and this will complete the circuit.

(5) When the battery, your switch and the bulb are connected, you can switch the light on and off (see diagram).

Using your new switch, you can make a code light. First make the circuit with the switch. Then make up a code based on long and short flashes. Now messages can be flashed across a darkened room. You could learn Morse code and send messages with that.

Let's find out how to light two or more torch bulbs at the same time

Things you will need
1½v battery
three small torch bulbs
three bulb holders
an electrician's screwdriver
several strands of thin electrical wire
three switches (you may want to make these yourself)

Now that you know how to make a simple circuit with a single bulb, put two or three bulbs into a circuit. Later, if you want to build a model house or garage, you can then make a circuit that gives a light for each room.

Make a simple circuit with three bulbs arranged in a row along one long line of wire (you will need four strands of wire to do this).

Connect the wires to the battery terminals so that the circuit is complete. What do you notice? All three bulbs dimly light up. This is because the bulbs are connected one after the other and the current going through each one is reduced.

Bulbs arranged like this in a circuit are *in series*. This type of circuit is not common because the light produced in the bulbs is too dull. If you build a model house with, say, seven rooms, and have the bulbs in series, the rooms would be almost too dark to use.

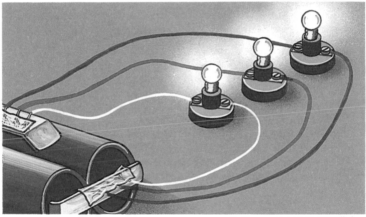

Bulbs arranged in parallel

There is another way to put bulbs into a circuit so that they all light up brightly.

What you do

(1) Make a circuit with a single bulb screwed into a bulb holder.

(2) When the bulb is lit, fix another two wires and bulb to the battery terminals and then another. Notice now that the bulbs are very bright. Bulbs arranged this way are *in parallel*.

(3) When you have made a parallel circuit, can you now put three switches into the circuit so that each bulb can be switched on and off without affecting the other two?

The problem with this design is that the battery is used up three times as fast because you have made three separate circuits. Is there another way of making a parallel circuit?

Let's find out how to make a nerve machine

This is a fun experiment and just the thing to make for parties to give your friends a challenge and a laugh.

Things you will need

3v battery	bulb and bulb holder
some thin wire	wire cutters
a wire coat hanger	Plasticine

What you do

(1) Cut a long piece of strong iron wire from an old coat hanger and bend it into a twisting, bendy, up and down shape. You might find it safer to wear gloves when you bend the wire so that you don't scratch yourself.

(2) Connect one end of the strong wire to a 3v battery. Connect a bulb to the battery.

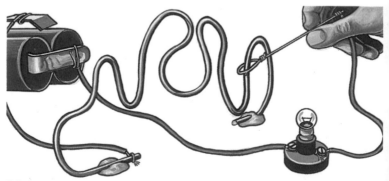

(3) Take another long strand of wire, fix it to a bulb terminal, and make a noose for the other end so that it surrounds the coat hanger wire. When the wire touches the coat hanger the circuit is completed and the light goes on (see diagram).

(4) Stick the coat hanger wire into a Plasticine base so that it doesn't fall over. Now test how steady your hand is. Can you hold the wire noose and move it up and down the wire without touching it and lighting the bulb?

This nerve machine is even more fun if you fix a bell into the circuit. You can buy a bell and this would be joined into the circuit in the same way as your bulb.

The electrician's shorthand

When electricians and scientists make new circuits they often follow diagrams written using special symbols. We can use symbols for our experiments which are similar to those used by experts.

Here are the signs:

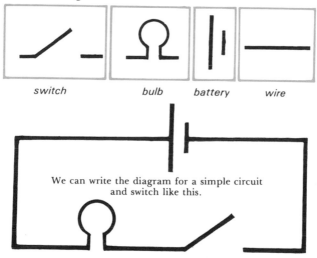

switch   bulb   battery   wire

We can write the diagram for a simple circuit
and switch like this.

31

Investigations with electricity

Can you make these circuits?

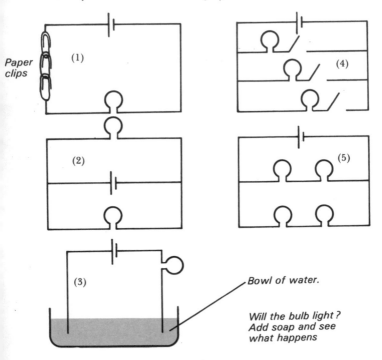

Paper clips

(1)

(2)

(3)

(4)

(5)

Bowl of water.

Will the bulb light?
Add soap and see
what happens

(6) Can you make a circuit with a 1½v battery, a bulb, a pen knife, and NOTHING ELSE?

(7) Can a circuit be made with string instead of wire?

(8) Can you light a bulb by connecting only one of the contacts in the holder?

(9) Will a switch work as well on either side of a light bulb in a circuit?

(10) Can you make a monster's face out of a cardboard box and give it a pair of flashing lights for eyes?

Let's find out what a battery is made from

The batteries in our experiments are normally used for lighting torches and bicycle lamps, and providing power for transistor radios. Batteries are small, powerful packages of electric energy. The more powerful the battery in a circuit, the larger the current it produces.

Scientists and electricians call the batteries we are using in our experiments, *primary cells* or *dry batteries*. These batteries supply a set amount of electricity and when that has been used, they cannot be recharged. What are they made of? You can easily find out if you have a worn-out battery.

Take the battery apart on a big sheet of newspaper because some of the inside parts can be rather messy. Have a rag or cloth close by to wipe your hands. If any of the contents of the cell get on your hands or clothes, wash it off straightaway in warm soapy water.

What you do

(1) Take off the cardboard wrapping until you come to a metal container. This is called the cell.

(2) Carefully take off the cell casing, which is made of zinc, with a pair of pliers. Inside you will see a soft, jelly-like substance round a black, sticky powder.

(3) Using the pliers carefully, firmly twist the brass cap at the top and pull. Out will come a long, thin, black rod made from carbon.

The carbon rod with the brass cap and the zinc case are the poles of the battery. The white jelly-like substance and the soft, black, sticky powder are chemicals which make electricity flow when the poles are connected to a circuit.

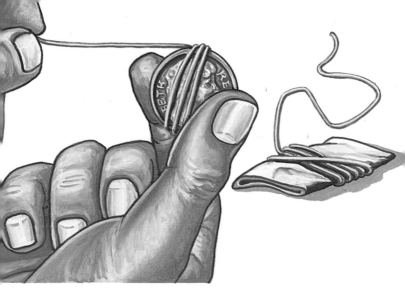

Let's find out how to make a battery

Things you will need
a coin
a jam jar
a torch bulb in a holder
strands of copper wire (available from electricians' shops)
two cupfuls of malt vinegar
the parts from an old battery

What you do
(1) Use the zinc casing from the bits of battery you took apart. Wash the zinc metal in warm soapy water, dry it and then rub it with fine sandpaper.
(2) Cut off two 15 cm lengths of copper wire and wind one round the zinc casing and the other round the coin (see picture above).
(3) Attach the ends of the wires to the bulb holder and put the coin and zinc casing into the empty jam jar.

(4) Pour in the vinegar and watch the bulb. It will flicker for a short time then light up quite brightly.

Electricity is produced in the jar and the current travels through the circuit into the bulb. How long does it last? Is it stronger than a 1½v battery?

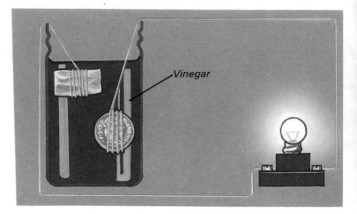

Vinegar

Lemons produce electricity

Citric acid gives lemons a sharp, tingling taste. Did you know that citric acid also produces electricity?

Let's find out
(1) Choose a large, firm, juicy lemon and roll it a few times on a table. Squeeze it hard to break some of the tissue inside the skin.
(2) Cut two slits in the lemon skin with a sharp knife and force in a piece of zinc casing and a carbon rod from an old battery. Make sure that these two don't touch each other under the lemon skin.
(3) Twist some copper wire round the carbon rod and another piece round the zinc and make a circuit with a small bulb. The lemon may produce enough electricity to light up the bulb.

Make sure
that the carbon rod
and the zinc casing
are not touching each other
inside the lemon

Don't be disappointed if it does not, because there is
another way of finding out if the lemon is producing a
current. Hold the wires that were attached to the bulb
against your tongue. You will feel a slight tickle because
your tongue is conducting the small amount of electricity
produced by the action of the acid in the lemon.

If your bulb didn't light, try two lemons with the wires
linked together.

Conductors and Insulators

When wire is connected correctly to a battery and a
bulb, the bulb lights. We have made a circuit. For this to
happen, however, the connecting wires must allow
electricity to pass through them.

Substances that electricity passes through easily are
called *conductors*. Those that do not are called *insulators*.

Let's find out which materials conduct electricity

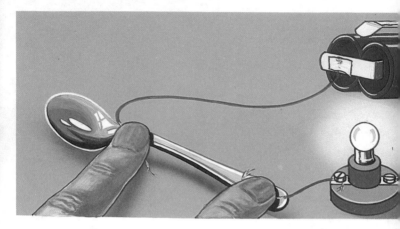

Things you will need

Some 'odds and ends' similar to those you collected for the experiment to discover which materials are attracted to a magnet (see page 6)

some lengths of wire
bulb holder
bulb
3v battery

What you do

(1) Begin by making a circuit with the battery, a bulb in a holder, and two strands of wire. When the circuit is complete and the bulb lights, cut one of the wires in the middle with the wire cutters.

(2) Bare the ends of the cut wire and, using both ends, touch one of the objects from the 'odds and ends' collection. If the bulb lights, then the material you put in the circuit is a good conductor.

(3) Try other materials.

Good conductors of electricity are metals like iron, copper and steel. Good insulators are non-metals like wood and rubber. There are exceptions, though.

Pencil lead (which is a graphite rod) is a good conductor of electricity. Did you test it?

Insulating electrical equipment is very important because it protects us from getting a shock when we switch on things like electric kettles or a television set. All electrical wires and switches that conduct household electric currents are covered in rubber or plastic. These substances are good insulators and stop the current from leaking.

Fuses

Fuses are safety devices. When too much current is flowing in a circuit the wires can melt and start a fire. There are lots of reasons why faults develop in circuits but the most common cause of problems is the *short circuit*. Short circuits happen when a new path is taken by the electric current, bypassing the bulb or gadget that you are operating. Short circuits sometimes occur when old wires lose their protective coverings. When the bare wires touch, the current shoots across, quickly heating the wire.

A fuse is thin wire made from metal which melts at low temperatures. So, if something does go wrong in a circuit, the short metal fuse wire melts, turns black and breaks in half. Immediately the circuit is broken and the electricity stops flowing and the danger of fire is prevented.

30 amp (x), 13 amp (y) and 3 amp (z) fuse wire and two fuse cartridges used in plugs

Let's find out how to make a fuse

Things you will need
4½v battery
bulb in bulb holder
switch
wire
steel wool

What you do
(1) Make a circuit with a battery, some wire and a bulb.
(2) Attach a thin fibre of steel wool to the end of one piece of wire and the bulb holder (see diagram).
(3) When the power is switched on, the steel wool quickly heats and melts. This breaks the circuit and the bulb goes out.

What other materials could be used as fuse wire?

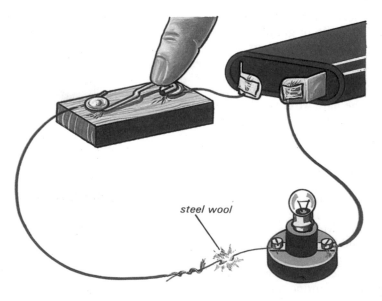

steel wool

Electricity for homes

Hydro-electric station at Henrik Verwoerd Dam on the Orange River in South Africa

Many home gadgets rely on electricity. Where does the power come from?

The television set is connected to the wall plug, in which there are wires linked to the meter box unit that tells how much electrical power we use at home. Meters receive current from a *distribution point* located near each home. Distribution points are connected to a *transformer* which is linked to the huge pylons we see towering above the countryside. The pylons support the power lines which are carriers of vast amounts of electric current from the *power stations* where the electricity is actually generated.

Some power stations are *hydro-electric* which means that the electricity is produced from the power of flowing water. Others are *nuclear power stations* and the electricity is created by heat from nuclear energy.

The electric light bulb

Look closely with a magnifying glass at one of your torch bulbs and a house light bulb. Can you see the fine metal strand of wire held in position by two heavier wires? The metal wire, or *filament,* is made of wolfram (once called tungsten). Wolfram is an ideal metal wire for bulbs because, as electricity passes through it, it soon gets hot, glows and gives off light.

The modern light bulb took a long time to develop. Our modern light bulb was created by Thomas Alva Edison (1847-1931) who lived in America. When he was twelve years old he left home and started working on the trains as a newsboy, taking newspapers and messages to the passengers. He was fascinated by science and did lots of experiments in his spare time. This got him into trouble with his employers because he did not concentrate on his work. Eventually, when he was a young man, he became an inventor and made the first talking picture, the microphone and the phonograph. He also designed an electric light bulb that would not burn out quickly; an idea that quickly became very popular in homes and factories.

Thomas Edison experiments in his home laboratory

Let's find out how to make a light bulb

Things you will need

5 cm *very* thin iron wire
small bottle or jar
thick card to make a lid for jar
2 long nails

materials to make a switch
2 batteries
wire

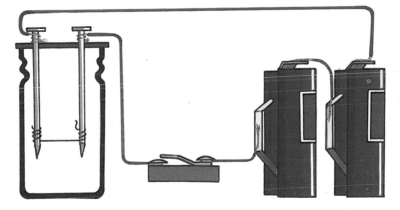

What you do

(1) Cut a piece of thick cardboard to make a cap for the
small bottle or jar.

(2) Press two nails through the card and fix your filament
across the two pointed ends. Fix the cardboard on the
bottle top.

(3) Join the wires to the heads of the nails, and to a
switch and two batteries connected together (see
diagram).

(4) When you switch on, the filament should glow red
hot. You may have to experiment to find the right
length of wire for the filament, but let it cool before
you touch it. It will burn away quickly, but a real
bulb contains a special gas to stop the filament
burning away.

Some more experiments

Electricity and Magnetism

Early in the 19th century a famous Danish scientist called Dr Oersted proved that there are similarities between electricity and magnetism. We can do Oersted's experiment using the compass that we made earlier (see page 15).

Things you will need
a home made compass
saucer of water
a bar magnet
30 cm of thin iron wire
1½ v battery
switch

What you do
(1) Hold a small bar magnet near the compass needle. The needle will turn on the water because the lines of force from the magnet attract it. When the magnet is taken away, the needle returns to the north/south direction.

(2) Now connect a 1½ v battery, a switch, and about 30 cm of iron wire, and fix the wire across the top of the saucer with Sellotape, in the same N/S direction as the needle.

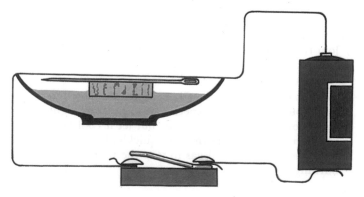

44

(3) Check all the connections and then switch on the current. The needle moves just as it did when the magnet was held near it. The electric current produces the same effect as a magnet.
This classic experiment was the beginning of the study and the use of *electromagnetism*.

(4) Repeat the experiment and use a lemon battery. What happens? Even though the current from the lemon is very small, it moves the compass needle.

Oersted's discovery led to the invention of the electromagnet. Today, huge electromagnets are used in heavy industry and scrapyards for lifting huge pieces of iron and steel. We can make a small electromagnet which will attract tiny metal objects like tacks and needles.

Let's find out how to make an electromagnet

Things you will need
4½v battery
a switch
a long length of plastic coated wire
a steel nail

What you do
(1) Wind about 60 turns of plastic covered wire round a long nail, leaving the bared ends free so that you can connect them to a 4½v battery and an on/off switch.

(2) Put the nail in the middle of a pile of paper clips or tacks and switch the power on. The nail will pick up the clips like a magnet and drop them immediately the power is switched off.

(3) If you use steel and not an iron nail, then the metal will stay permanently magnetised when the current is switched off.

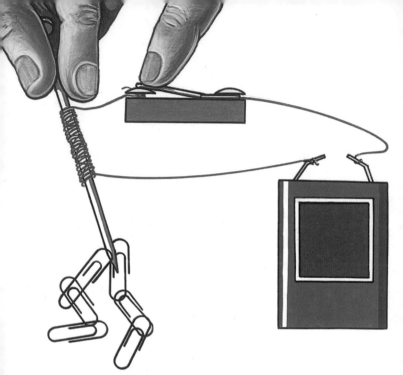

(4) Put two batteries in the circuit. Does it make your electromagnet stronger?

You will discover that the more turns of wire round the steel nail, then the stronger the magnet.

Electric Motors

Michael Faraday (1791-1867) made the first electric motor. Faraday's primitive electric motor was the forerunner of today's incredibly powerful motors that drive buses, cars, milk carts, trains and machines throughout the world.

We can make a simple working model of an electric motor.

Making a pin and cork electric motor

Things you will need
1 large cork (the size used in wine making)
some drawing pins
thin wire coated with plastic
a 4½v battery
a piece of soft wood (eg balsa) measuring 10 cm by 15 cm
a long darning needle
some pins
a large horseshoe magnet with a gap of about 35 mm between
the two poles
OR 3 bar magnets

What you do

Our model electric motor will have an *armature* (the
section that moves round) and a base. Make the armature
first.

(1) Cut two grooves, lengthways, down opposite sides of
the cork and then hold it tightly in a pair of pliers
and push a darning needle right through the middle
from end to end. This is not very easy so take your
time. Wear a thimble so that you don't stick the
needle in your finger.

(2) When you have done it, spin the cork between your
fingers to make sure that the needle has gone exactly
through the middle of the cork. This is important.

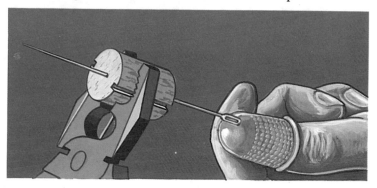

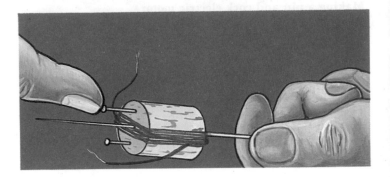

(3) Wind the thin wire on the grooved cork, leaving the two bared ends. When you have done this, stick the two pins in the cork the same distance apart on each side of the needle. Leave about 1 cm of each pin sticking out.

(4) Wrap one end of the wire tightly round one of the pins to make a firm connection. Twist the other end round the other pin. The armature is now completed so put it to one side for awhile.

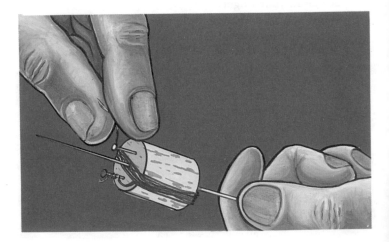

(5) To make the base you need a piece of wood about 15 cm long and about 10 cm wide, and soft enough to stick drawing pins in.

(6) Stick a pair of pins at each end, crossed so that they can support the darning needle running through the cork. Test and see if the armature rotates freely when it is resting on the crossed pins. (Two small strips of card glued to the wood, the correct distance apart, will stop the needle from sliding to and fro.)

(7) Connect the two wires that take current to the armature. These are called *brushes* because they brush against the two pins as the armature spins round. The brushes are the bared ends of wires which stick up and are fixed in place by two drawing pins in the wooden board. The other ends of these two wires are connected to a 4½v battery.

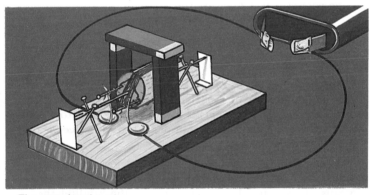

The completed motor

(8) Put a strong horseshoe magnet over the armature, check that all the connections are secure, and give your cork and pin motor a spin to start it off. If everything is right, the cork armature should continue to spin as long as the wires are connected to the battery. Try using three bar magnets in a U shape if you cannot obtain a large horseshoe magnet.

Useful facts about electricity

Measurement of voltage and current

Voltage from batteries is measured by an instrument called a *voltmeter*. Voltmeters are expensive instruments but you may be lucky enough to come across one in a junk shop. If you can manage to get one, connect wire to it and fix the bare ends to a battery. The needle will indicate the voltage (electrical force) coming from the battery. If you use a 4v battery for this experiment, the needle will not necessarily point to the 4v mark because if the battery has been used before, the electrical force will reduce.

A voltmeter can be connected to a circuit with a bulb to show what voltage is forcing the current through it.

Current is measured by an *ammeter*. The current is the same wherever it is measured in a circuit.

Conductors of electricity

Silver is the best conductor of electricity.

Pure water (that is, rain water and distilled water) is a very bad conductor of electricity BUT dirty bath water (the dirt particles carry current) is a very good conductor. This is why there are careful precautions taken over electrical fittings in a bathroom.

A long wire in a circuit will need a bigger force than a short wire needs to make the same current flow. That means, the shorter the wire in a circuit the brighter the light from the bulb.

Electricity will flow into the ground by whatever path is easiest. Appliances have, for protection, a wire fixed to the earth pin of the plug so that if a fault develops, the electricity will go into the plug and then into the ground, and not through us!

If a wire became faulty in a machine like a hair dryer that was not earthed, the electricity would flow through the person using it and into the ground, giving a nasty electric shock.

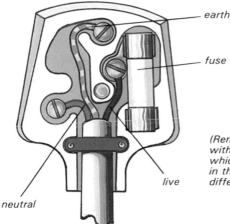

earth

fuse

(Remember to check with your electricity shop which fuse you should have in the plug for each different appliance)

live

neutral

BE SAFE AND SURE WHEN USING ELECTRICITY

Remember, that even though electricity is man's servant it can also **kill**.

Remember these rules

1 Never play with power points.
2 Never use a gadget that has damaged wires.
3 Never use an appliance when your hands are wet.
4 Never use an appliance in the bathroom.
5 Never overload a circuit.
6 Never fly a kite near telephone wires or power lines.
7 Never play with a car battery.
8 Never try to repair anything which uses mains electricity.

INDEX